# SEOUL

## THE CITY AT A GLANC

GW00771468

### N Seoul Tower

Revamped and reimagined in 2
glitzed-up facilities and a new r
Tower remains the city's definir
*See p010*

### Seoul Museum of Art (SeMA)

Located in this 1927, former Supreme
Court building, SeMA boasts a visit-worthy
permanent collection of works by Korean
artists, from painting to calligraphy.
*30 Misulgwangil, 37 Seosomun-dong,
Jung-gu, T 2124 8800*

### Namdaemun Market

Folksy crafts, food, fashion – it's all here in
this centuries-old market open for business
around the clock. Search out the stalls set
up by Seoul's young graduate designers.
*See p080*

### Namsan Park

Sloping up Mount Namsan and down to
Myeong-dong, this park is a verdant pleasure
ground packed with attractions, from the
National Theatre to the Paljakjung pavilion.
*100-177 Hoehyun-dong 1-ga, Jung-gu,
T 2753 2563*

### JoongAng Ilbo building

The founder of Samsung, Lee Byung-chul,
was also the first publisher of one of South
Korea's major dailies, the right-leaning
*JoongAng Ilbo*, produced here since 1965.
*7 Sunhwa-dong, Jung-gu*

### Seoul Station

Fans of high-speed train travel head to the
city's main rail hub, where they can hop on the
KTX, South Korea's answer to the bullet train.
*43-205 Dongja-dong, Yongsan-gu, T 2392 1324*

# INTRODUCTION
## THE CHANGING FACE OF THE URBAN SCENE

Though the South Korean government might like to pat itself on the back for prime-time city branding during the 1988 Summer Olympics and the 2002 FIFA World Cup, it was a more organic set of circumstances that put this full-on city on the global map. Seoul has pulled off the neat trick of becoming the dominant pop culture influence in Asia – even luring the fan base of its great rival Japan – and combined this with a knack for big business and cutting-edge design and technology. Now, the city doesn't just produce the Far East's soap stars, film actors and musicians, which are plastered all over billboards from Beijing to Bangkok, it also supplies the TVs and gadgets on which people watch, listen to, talk about, transmit, record and replay them. And for every giant such as Samsung and LG, there's now an upstart like INNO Design (see p081) or MMMG (153 Anguk-dong, Jongno-gu, T 3210 1604); for every K-pop heart-throb, there's an art-house cinema.

The big hotel brands such as Hyatt, W and Ritz-Carlton have flocked to the city, while homegrown classics, such as The Shilla (see p016), have upped their game with stylish renovations. These days, architects of the calibre of Jean Nouvel and Rem Koolhaas arrive at immigration beside the curious tourists. What they'll find is a city of extremes, led by a visionary mayor, Oh Se-hoon, and culture and energy to burn. Seoul's transformation has not been easy, but then few predicted it would ever make it this far.

# ESSENTIAL INFO
## FACTS, FIGURES AND USEFUL ADDRESSES

**TOURIST OFFICE**
*KTO building*
*40 Cheonggyecheonno*
*Jung-gu*
*T 729 9497*
*english.tour2korea.com*

**TRANSPORT**
**Car hire**
Hertz
*107-1 Nonhyeon-dong*
*Gangnam-gu*
*T 3443 8000*
**Taxis**
Deluxe Taxis
*Shincheon-dong*
*Songpa-gu*
*T 3431 5100*

**EMERGENCY SERVICES**
**Ambulance/Fire**
*T 119*
**Police**
*T 112*
**24-hour pharmacy**
Jeil Grand Pharmacy
*200 Nonhyeon-dong*
*Gangnam-gu*
*T 549 7451*

**EMBASSIES**
**British Embassy**
*40 Taepyungro*
*4 Jeong-dong*
*Jung-gu*
*T 3210 5500*
*www.britishembassy.or.kr*
**US Embassy**
*32 Sejongno*
*Jongno-gu*
*T 397 4114*
*seoul.usembassy.gov*

**MONEY**
**American Express**
*T 399 2929*
*travel.americanexpress.com*

**POSTAL SERVICES**
**Post Office**
*1 Banporo*
*Jung-gu*
*T 6450 1114*
**Shipping**
UPS
*159 Coex Shopping Mall*
*Samsung-dong*
*Kangnam-gu*
*T 6002 6886*

**BOOKS**
**Flowers of a Moment** by Ko Un
(BOA Editions)
**Korea's Place in the Sun** by Bruce Cumings
(WW Norton & Co)

**WEBSITES**
**Magazine**
*www.koreana.or.kr*
**Newspapers**
*www.seouldaily.com*
*www.theseoultimes.com*

**COST OF LIVING**
**Taxi from Incheon International**
**Airport to city centre**
£40
**Cappuccino**
£3.75
**Packet of cigarettes**
£1.35
**Daily newspaper**
£0.70
**Bottle of champagne**
£70

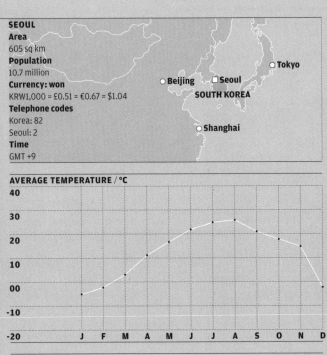

**SEOUL**
**Area**
605 sq km
**Population**
10.7 million
**Currency: won**
KRW1,000 = £0.51 = €0.67 = $1.04
**Telephone codes**
Korea: 82
Seoul: 2
**Time**
GMT +9

Tokyo

Beijing　☐ Seoul
**SOUTH KOREA**

Shanghai

**AVERAGE TEMPERATURE / °C**

| | | | | | | | | | | | |
|---|---|---|---|---|---|---|---|---|---|---|---|
40
30
20
10
00
-10
-20

J F M A M J J A S O N D

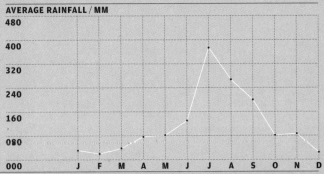

**AVERAGE RAINFALL / MM**

480
400
320
240
160
080
000

J F M A M J J A S O N D

# NEIGHBOURHOODS
## THE AREAS YOU NEED TO KNOW AND WHY

To help you navigate the city, we've chosen the most interesting districts (see below and the map inside the back cover) and colour-coded our featured venues, according to their location; those venues that are outside these areas are not coloured.

### MYEONG-DONG

Financial oomph meets consumerism in this hectic hub. A host of big players roost here in a quirky collection of buildings that range from the Western-inspired colonial City Hall (see p009) to the post-industrial Jongno Tower (see p012). The something-for-everyone atmosphere draws corporate suits, high-end shoppers and skateboard punks, but it's distinctly not a late-night area beyond the local *bulgogi* (marinated beef) and *soju* (rice wine) bars.

### APGUJEONG

This wild, eclectic and youthful district is home to art-house cinemas and UN Studio's Galleria shopping mall (see p014). However, the real action is in the area's backstreets, which buzz with denim-clad twentysomethings and helter-skelter neon signage. Here, concept stores sell everything from motorcycles to French fries to fedoras. It's a great place to experience the fun spirit of K-culture.

### SAMCHEONG-DONG

This still-emerging district wears a leafy, residential cloak, curving around the genteel grounds of Gyeongbokgung Palace (see p033) and buffered by the ancient homes of Bukcheon, one of the few remaining swathes of prewar buildings. Leading the re-emergence of the northern part of the city, its cutting-edge galleries and shops, moody bistros and all-hours cafés have given it real cachet.

### HONGDAE

In urban development terms, Seoul got ahead of itself by creating a dynamic district in the 'burbs before similar areas developed in the city centre. Hongdae is a youthful 1990s-Brooklyn-gone-Korean, with low-cost living, artistic flair, impromptu clubs and a wild temperament. There's no sign of it slowing down, thanks to anchors such as the Hongik University Faculty of Fine Arts and cultural centre Ssamzie Space (5-129 Changjeon-dong, T 3142 1695).

### ITAEWON

Just down the hill from the Grand Hyatt (see p026) and Mount Namsan is what was once a firmly expat quarter of embassies, US army barracks and English teachers. But in the past two years, the demographic has changed and a small, vibrant cluster of 24-hour cafés, posh lounges, gay clubs and restaurants, such as Above Bar (see p058), has emerged. Now, Itaewon is fast becoming a destination in its own right.

### CHEONGDAM-DONG

Crowded with packs of black BMWs waiting to pick up their high-wattage charges from Gucci, Hermès and Armani, this is Seoul's answer to Beverly Hills. Tucked behind the brand temples and Westernised coffee emporia are the snaking alleys where the high-rollers live, while the lower reaches are a magnet for small nightspots, such as S Bar (see p056) and Miss Park (see p059), and chichi bistros of every description.

# LANDMARKS
## THE SHAPE OF THE CITY SKYLINE

Navigating Seoul is a challenge for visitor and resident alike, and it's de rigueur to get a map of your destination before you head out anywhere. Neatly snipping this massive capital in two is the Han River. The northern side, Hangbuk, houses many of the older, more pastoral districts. Walker Hill is a hiker's paradise at the weekend and is crowned by the glass-sheeted W Seoul (see p028). Commanding terrific views from the top of another of the city's hills, the N Seoul Tower (overleaf) marks the heart of the Mount Namsan area – home to the buzzy Itaewon and the Grand Hyatt hotel (see p026). The robotic-looking Jongno Tower (see p012) functions as a gateway to the dense Financial District, which is home to City Hall (31 Daepyeongno 1-ga, Jung-gu, T 120), the stock exchange and numerous department stores. North of this, the ancient Gyeongbokgung Palace (see p033) sits at the foot of an area encompassing the jagged alleys and winding streets of Bukcheon, art galleries and the fast-rising café scene of Samcheong-dong.

Heading south of the river, the Sun-Yu Pedestrian Arch Bridge looks across to the area where much of the city goes to work and play, and where life focuses almost exclusively on Seoul's sacred Cs: commerce and consumers. Here is the LCD-clad Galleria (see p014), whose location straddles the busy streets of Apgujeong and the 9021-gone-Korean avenues of Cheongdam-dong.

*For full addresses, see Resources.*

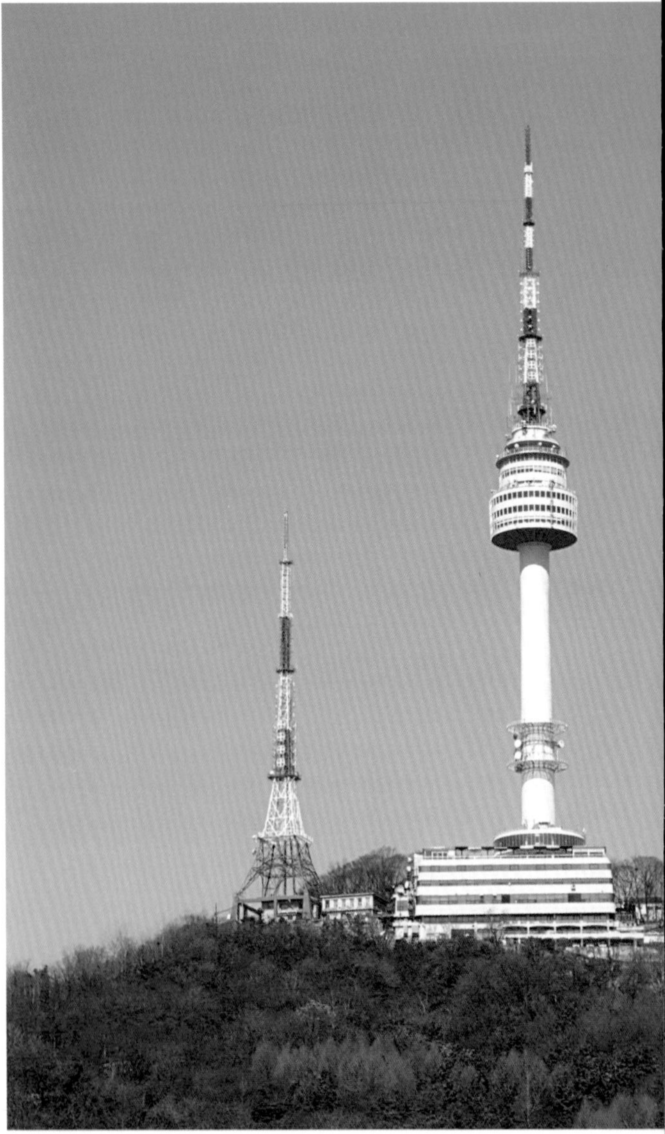

## N Seoul Tower

A slim, reed-like structure, perched on the peak of Mount Namsan, this 237m tower, completed in 1969, is equal parts visual cue and tourist spot. Renovations in 2005 saw a major redesign of the public spaces and a renaming of the tower, to include an 'N', for Namsan. The elevated section, dubbed the Observation Zone, features the viewing deck, offering stunning 360-degree views, now enhanced via high-tech 'digitalised binoculars', a revolving restaurant and a café. At the base of the tower, a plaza area hosts cultural events and exhibitions. In an effort to protect the mountain, private cars were banned in 2005, but the tower is easily accessible via bus or taxi. Or you could really do your bit for the environment and walk up there, following one of the trails leading through the leafy Namsan Park.
*San 1-3 Yongsan-dong 2-ga, Yongsan-gu, T 3455 9277, www.nseoultower.com*

**Jongno Tower**

This post-industrial landmark looming over Jongno, one of Seoul's major east-west arteries, is certainly at the modern end of the city's extremes. Clad in glass and latticed metal, it has a futuristic feel and, fittingly, nestles between old and new Seoul: the cobblestoned streets of arty Insadong and the high-rises of financial zone Myeong-dong. Rafael Viñoly Architects inherited a pre-exisiting frame when they won the competition, held in 1994, to redesign and finish the structure, which opened as a mixed-use building in 1999. It's worth zipping up to the Top Cloud bar/grill (T 2230 3000) on the 33rd floor, if only for fabulous views of the city through floor-to-ceiling windows.

*1-1 Jongno 2-ga, Jung-gu*

## Hyundai Development Company

The HQ for Hyundai's development arm was given its bold façade by architects Daniel Libeskind, working with local studio Himma. Named the 'Tangent', the 62m-diameter aluminium ring, 'hovering' on the glass curtain wall, is, according to Libeskind, intended to represent the circle of nature, and the diagonal vector cutting through the side of the building, technology; it also serves as a material link between the building and public plaza below. The balance that Libeskind believes should be struck between the two – nature and machine – is the point here.

*160-12, 15, 16 Samsung-dong, Kangnam-gu*

## Galleria

Designed by Dutch architects UN Studio,
and poised on a busy intersection, the
Galleria shopping mall acts as a gateway
to Apgujeong and Cheongdam-dong.
Its unmissable exterior – an intense,
pulsating, iridescent shell of LCD discs,
falls somewhere between sensual fish
scales and cartoonish snakeskin.
*494 Apgujeong-dong, Gangnam-gu,
T 3449 4114*

# HOTELS

## WHERE TO STAY AND WHICH ROOMS TO BOOK

When compared to other North-East Asian economic players (Tokyo and Beijing), travel hubs (Singapore and Hong Kong) and lifestyle playgrounds (Bangkok), the accommodation on offer in Seoul is a little lacking. Many hotels are business behemoths, such as the Millennium Hilton (see p020), and few have the much sought-after combination of location, style and excellent service found so easily in other big cities. But recent years have seen some changes.

Slightly out of the city, on Walker Hill, the W Seoul (see p028) has an urban-resort feel and serious retro-spunk; the concierges are also superb. The COEX business and shopping complex got an injection of design savvy when Park Hyatt (opposite) checked in with its first Korean property, whose awkward layout is saved by suave rooms, a 24th-floor pool with floor-to-ceiling windows, a fitness centre and Seoul's best bathrooms. Among the established players, the Grand Hyatt (see p026) has a regal, wood-clad lobby and lovely setting amid the verdant hills of Mt Namsan.

Meanwhile, Fraser Suites (72 Nakwon-dong, Jongno-gu, T 6262 8888) delivers efficiency and style among the ancient teahouses of Insadong, and two classics have recently been made over: The Shilla (202 Jangchung-dong 2-ga, Jung-gu, T 2233 3131) and Westin Chosun (87 Sogong-dong, Jung-gu, T 771 0500), whose public spaces and restaurants have been renovated by Adam Tihany. *For full addresses and room rates, see Resources.*

### Park Hyatt

Designed by Super Potato, the Park Hyatt displays many of the Tokyo firm's signatures: juxtaposition of wood and stone, clean, ultra-modern lines and amber lighting. The layout can be dizzying (the lobby, above, is on the 24th floor) but the rooms are arguably the most striking in the city: Myanmar oak-lined and with superb granite tubs and rain showers; the Diplomatic Suite (overleaf) also has a Bang & Olufsen sound system. Dining options include the hidden sushi counter in the basement Timber House (see p052), a whisky bar-cum-country home with live jazz, or the Italianate Cornerstone grill. Other pluses include spectacular views from the top-floor fitness centre and the hotel's location next to the COEX centre.
*995-14 Daechi 3-dong, Kangnam-gu, T 2016 1234, www.seoul.park.hyatt.com*

Diplomatic Suite, Park Hyatt

**Millennium Hilton**
Located at the base of Mount Namsan,
the Millennium Hilton has all the bells
and whistles of a luxury hotel, from the
striking lobby (right) and Seven Luck
Casino to a business centre with eight
meeting rooms. There are nearly as many
restaurants, including pan-Asian culinary
playground Orangerie and Il Ponte, which
hosts its lavish Cena dei Reali (Dinner
for Royalty) four times a year. The rooms,
such as the Executive 'e' Room (above),
are a different story, containing a mixed
bag of nondescript furnishings, but
the views of the mountainside from the
picture windows compensate. The hotel's
location also means you can skip the
standard hotel gym in favour of a bracing
uphill jog. Plus it's only a short stroll to
the hip wine bar Naos Nova (see p042)
and the N Seoul Tower (see p010).
*395 Namdaemun-ro 5-ga, Jung-gu,*
*T 753 7788, www.hilton.co.kr*

### Somerset Palace

If not quite a palace, then certainly a home away from home, the Somerset is a modern haven for frequent travellers to Seoul. Its serviced apartments, such as the One-Bedroom Executive (above), are custom-designed, earth-toned bubbles of comfort, while the rooftop offers myriad amenities, from attractive gardens, a pool and jacuzzi to barbecue equipment. A billiards room, a library lounge, a sauna and another garden at the back of the hotel are further attractions. The list of services is equally impressive: secretaries, couriers, chauffeurs, AV technicians and babysitters are available, in addition to the usual roster of hotel staff. Conveniently located, you can step out of Somerset Palace's cool marble lobby (opposite) into the heart of Seoul's diplomatic district and the galleries and antiques stores of Insadong.
*85 Susong-dong, Jongno-gu, T 6730 8888,*
*www.somerset.com*

### Imperial Palace

Opulent and outlandish, no expense was spared to renovate this decadent luxury hotel, from the soaring lobby with its patterned marble floor to the sumptuous European-style furnishings of its wildly carpeted rooms, awash with gold tones, and bathrooms with automated bidets. The Royal Suite (left) comes with a canopied king-sized bed, a grand piano and a large sunken tub overlooking the river, as well as a formal dining room. Three full-service restaurants include the Japanese eaterie Man Yo, while the nightclub, Zoë Bar, appears caught in a time machine, shuttling between ancient Greece, baroque-era Europe and Midtown Manhattan circa 1985. A small shopping arcade caters for distinguished gentlemen and ladies rather than edgy hipsters.
*248-7 Nonhyeon-dong, Kangnam-gu, T 3440 8000, www.imperialpalace.co.kr*

**Grand Hyatt**

There's an epic sweep to the way the city tumbles beneath this hotel, which stands proud on Mount Namsan amid 18 acres of landscaped gardens and waterfalls. We recommend booking a Grand Club Room (above), as the standard rooms are small, but even if you don't stay, the numerous lounges – indoors, outdoors, with a disco here and a greenhouse there, as well as pool and karaoke – are worth a look.

Come lunchtime, Seoul's high society flocks to the Grand Hyatt's many eateries. The seasoned service here includes bar staff who know how to make a proper martini, and if drinks lead to dinner, The Chinese Restaurant is the place to head.
*747-7 Hannam 2-dong, Yongsan-ku,*
*T 797 1234, seoul.grand.hyatt.com*

## The Ritz-Carlton

It's outside the main city hub, but this hotel remains a draw for visitors. The lobby (above) is a towering monument to marble and the rooms are cream-toned bastions of luxury, boasting serene views of the Seoul skyline, Frette sheets and deep soaking tubs. Granted, they're also shoeboxes, so opt for a Prime Deluxe, or even the Presidential Suite, with its artwork by Roy Lichtenstein and Picasso.

The Ritz Bar is a favourite haunt of the local financiers, while the Hanazono sashimi restaurant impresses with its picturesque Japanese garden setting, designed by Tachiko Koike. Surprisingly, less impressive is the hotel's service, which runs counter to the Ritz reputation and can at times border on the surly.
*602 Yeoksam-dong, Kangnam-gu,*
*T 3451 8000, www.ritzcarlton.com*

**W Seoul**
Featuring a chic, retro-futuristic design
by Studio GAIA, the W is arguably
the sexiest hotel in town. The exterior
is all polka-dot blue glass and there's
something very pop art about the lobby
and Living Room (overleaf). Choose
the Cool Corner Room (pictured) for its
circular king-sized bed and great views.
*21 Gwangjang-dong, Gwangjin-gu,
T 465 2222, www.starwoodhotels.com*

# 24 HOURS

## SEE THE BEST OF THE CITY IN JUST ONE DAY

The city's seething traffic and round-the-clock appetite for work, drink and food make it very much a patchwork urban experience. As such, cars, subways and a good bit of shoe leather are necessary to cram everything into 24 hours. By day, this means centring your efforts on the north side of the river, where watching the morning light shimmer into focus from the soaring lobby of the Grand Hyatt (see p026) is a fitting start to a day in this most Eastern of cities.

When the traffic abates a little, head to the gentle, rolling hills and calming expanse of Gyeongbokgung Palace (opposite), where the secret gardens, quirky museums and history trip help right impressions of what can at times seem an extremely ugly city. A pleasant stroll away are two art galleries (see p034) that reveal an interesting reaction to the speed of Korea's modernisation; both extreme and expressive. From here, juggle your itinerary as you wish, as the sloping roofs of Bukcheon, the wine bars and coffee shops of Samcheong-dong and the craft-filled alleys of Insadong run in a gentle curve up the hill of the palace and back around behind the US Embassy (32 Sejongno, Jongno-gu).

After dark, head south of the river, to Bamboo House (658-10 Yeoksam-dong, Gangnam-gu, T 555 6390) for superb sirloin, pine mushrooms and crab roe served by a knowing, joyful staff. Then, until sleep strikes, it's off to the cavernous club, Circle (see p038). *For full addresses, see Resources.*

**10.00** Gyeongbokgung Palace

Understated elegance and bold lines characterise this iconic palace at the centre of northern Seoul's revival. Mountains rise to its north, where the official presidential residence, Cheongwadae (T 737 5800), or the Blue House, is nestled, while the ultra-urban Samcheong-dong and Bukcheon districts curl beyond its walls to the east. The stone pagodas, some of which are as tall as 10 storeys, are among the original elements that survived the 16th-century Japanese invasion. The internal gardens are uniformly excellent, demonstrating a skill in the creation of shapes and use of space that is uniquely Korean. Also on site is the National Folk Museum (T 3704 3114), whose 25,000 artefacts documenting Korean culture and everyday life are well worth a 30-minute detour.

*1 Sejong-no, Jongno-gu, T 734 2457*

**12.00 Kukje and Hyundai galleries**
Just outside the Gyeongbokgung Palace walls (see p033) lies a strip of striking, concrete-and-glass buildings that helped to propel Korean art onto the global stage. Kukje Gallery (left) and Gallery Hyundai continue their roles as best-in-class, where visitors are just as likely to see cutting-edge Western talents (Damien Hirst, Cy Twombly, Ed Ruscha) as Korean installations and video art pieces.

Downstairs from the Kukje Gallery, the Cafe (T 735 8441; above) is a great sit-and-sip or grab-and-go spot for a green-tea latte and macaroon or pressed sandwich. *Kukje Gallery, 59-1 Sogyeok-dong, Jongno-gu, T 735 8449, www.kukjegallery.com; Gallery Hyundai, 80 Sagan-dong, Jongno-gu, T 734 6111, www.galleryhyundai.com*

**15.00 Arario Gallery**
Continuing the art trail, Arario Gallery
showcases a mix of Chinese and Korean
talents, such as Inbai Kim (installation,
pictured), and is set back on a small lane
filled with noodle shops. Head on up the
hill to hidden gem Samcheong-dong and
its ceramics studios, cobblers, milliners
and ever-changing roster of wine bars.
*149-2 Sogyeok-dong, Jongno-gu,*
*T 723 6190, www.ararioseoul.com*

**20.00** Circle

It's time to head south of the river. Stop off for a tender beef steak and *banchan* (assorted side dishes) from the Korean barbecue at Bamboo House (see p032), before heading to nearby Circle. Big club openings are few and far between in generally conservative Seoul, so the arrival of this venue was a major event. Featuring a creative lighting scheme and some sleek geometrics, Circle is less imposing than some of Asia's so-called superclubs. A circular bar dominates the room, surrounded by a dancefloor, rows of bed-sized banquettes and a VIP area. Blue, pink and black light emanates from beneath bar tops and from behind the soft panelled walls. Beware, after-hours culture is still in its infancy in Seoul, and clubbers' awkwardness early on in the evening often gives way to wild, drunken dancing.
*91-2 Cheongdam-dong, Kangnam-gu, T 546 5933*

# URBAN LIFE
## CAFÉS, RESTAURANTS, BARS AND NIGHTCLUBS

Seoul's work-driven culture and nine-to-nine office hours mean that, to many visitors, the city appears a straight-laced place. Certainly, it is no Tokyo, Hong Kong or Bangkok, but beneath its traditional exterior a 'scene' has begun to take shape. It has been a phased phenomenon that has tended to concentrate on single-concept venues. Urbane cafés, whose slick interiors attract A-list media players and their latte habit cluster in Samcheong-dong and Apgujeong, while the upmarket Cheongdam-dong is the centre of the city's emerging bistro-and-grill culture, including Manhattan-inspired concepts such as Tribeca (89-6 Cheongdam-dong, Kangnam-gu, T 3448 4550). While back-street *soju* parlours and their beery/diner-like counterparts, *hofs*, are still a must-do-once Korean experience, wine has become the new tipple of choice. The likes of Vinga (see p051) boast certified sommeliers, while it-spots such as Tutto Bene (118-9 Cheongdam-dong, Kangnam-gu, T 546 1489) offer a laid-back atmosphere and eclectic surrounds.

After-dark crawls tend to veer from hotel bars, such as The Timber House (see p052), to karaoke joints, and from BBQs, such as Bamboo House (see p032), to the slowly rising number of dance clubs, such as Club Mass (137-074 Dae-dong B/D, 1306-8 Seocho-dong, Seocho-gu, T 599 3165) and M2 (367-11 Seogyo-dong, Mapo-gu, T 3143 7573), where DJ culture has just come into vogue. *For full addresses, see Resources.*

### The Gaon

Designed by Super Potato, this three-storey paean to the glories of traditional Korean cookery achieves something few others have: the marriage of contemporary design and culinary rusticity. Each floor here has its own look; the second level in particular shines. The company that owns The Gaon also manufactures tableware, so diners' food is sent out on plates that you may find yourself wanting to purchase.

Celebrity chef Yoon Jung-jin turns out winners such as *kimchi* stew, vegetable pancakes, pork belly and whole chicken simmered with red ginseng.
*631-23 Sinsa-dong, Kangnam-gu,*
*T 3446 8411*

### Naos Nova

Fashion designer-turned-restaurateur
Kyle Lee hired architect Jeon Shi-hyong
to craft a sculpture-dotted three-storey
space that's all angular steel, glass and
smooth concrete, offset by black-and-
white furniture. A timber-decked rooftop
bar and café boasts some striking views
of the surrounding urban patchwork,
consisting of tiny, slope-roofed homes,
1970s-era tenements, five-star hotels and
rising office towers. Part of a spate of
development around Mount Namsan that
brought the northern side of the river into
its own, Naos Nova is a little quiet now,
but the high-wattage set still descends
after work for the right bottle of Côtes
du Rhône or Opus One. The menu ranges
from *panini* and char-grilled ribeyes
to chocolate confections.
*448-120 Huam-dong, Yongsan-gu,*
*T 754 2202, www.naosnova.com*

### Bar 19

The quiet but steady rise of the Garosugil area is evident in the host of boutiques that young fashion designers are opening up, and the influx of owner-run bistros, coffee shops and lounges. Bar 19 is one of the more pitch-perfect examples, a boxy affair that radiates low-key chic with its mix-and-match wooden furniture, windows that open onto the street and a soupçon of clunky, modern Chinese flair.

Gathering steam after 10pm, the crowd, which tends towards artists and designers (though the buzz about the area is drawing curious parties of all types), lingers well into the night with the aid of DJs. Wine and mixed drinks are the libations of choice, brought by servers whose chattiness only furthers the bar's pub-like appeal.
*545-19 Sinsa-dong, Kangnam-gu,*
*T 543 4319*

## Actually

What actually is Actually? During the day, it's a coffee shop, offering a smattering of snacks, along with java, that puts the stuff served up by the chains to shame – its talented *baristas* brew some of the best espressos and cappuccinos in Seoul. By night, it dims the lights, ups the music volume, increases the menu options and becomes a fully fledged lounge. The designers cut a chunk out of a cement block, added nooks, crannies and a tiny terrace and made Actually a cool and stylish – yet comfortable – place to chill. You don't have to scream to be heard here, and the menu is fun, running from peanut butter-and-jelly sandwiches to light mains. *118-1 Cheongdam-dong, Kangnam-gu, T 3445 1350*

### Ariake

Achingly calm but for its drama queen's dream of an entrance staircase, the Japanese dining room in The Shilla hotel (see p016) is a picture of serenity, with its smooth woodwork and simple lines. The servers are equally gentle and beautifully put together. As at any quality Japanese eaterie, and this is one of Seoul's best, the prices can enter the stratosphere, but the value for money is indisputable. The simplicity paramount to the cuisine, but so deceptively hard to achieve, is the house speciality. The sashimi, tempura and sushi are impeccable, and there's a fine selection of Korean and Japanese spirits.
*2nd floor, The Shilla, 202 Jangchung-dong 2-ga, Jung-gu, T 2230 3356*

**Diner Kraze**
This chain is a slightly more upscale version of the Kraze Burger franchise, with a design that is fun and arty, a kind of fast-food industrial chic. The surprisingly fresh and sometimes healthy menu also includes steak, pasta and rice dinners, although like everything else in Seoul, it's not cheap.
*87-4 Cheongdam-dong, Kangnam-gu,*
*T 546 0882*

## Café Mou

To the non-local, the Park View building appears to occupy a nondescript stretch of pavement near a few open swathes of grass. But it's actually the centre of Dosan Park, which has become a hot spot for upper-crust lunches and shopping trips by day, casual-chic family gatherings and the pre-club get-togethers of small but boozy groups of young women by night. A favourite among Seoul's A-listers, Café

Mou hosts the equivalent of café society. An open, high-ceilinged room reveals Asian influences and the background of its florist owner, with its blend of dark hardwoods and tree branches scattered throughout. *650-9 Park View building, Sinsa-dong, Gangnam-gu, T 3444 6069, www.cafemou.co.kr*

## Vinga

Save your drinking for when you get to Vinga – actually finding and entering this combined wine and sushi bar requires a clear head, located as it is down a steep staircase in the basement of a faceless building. Once you get there, however, you can relax: it's a lovely space, wide-open and airy, despite its subterranean setting, and decorated with lots of stone and wood as well as bottle racks (which aren't, however, so showy as to give you the feeling you're in a retail shop). A handsome wooden counter lets you rub shoulders while indulging in sips and nibbles. The wine selection is broad and interesting, as is the food menu.
*634-1 Sinsa-dong, Kangnam-gu, T 516 1761*

**The Timber House**
The main bar in the Park Hyatt (see p017) is a quirky juxtaposition of log cabin, jazz joint and sushi restaurant, frequented by corporate heavy-hitters and Prada-clad power couples. The clever interior design melds a mix of furnishings, from plush plaid chairs to slick bar stools and latticed screens.
*Park Hyatt, 995-14 Daechi 3-dong, Kangnam-gu, T 2016 1291*

### Gramercy Kitchen

Confidently cool and swanky, this outpost of The Westin Chosun (see p016) in the MJ building in the trendy district of Sinsa-dong is a meeting ground for Seoul's thirtysomething movers and shakers. Dark woods and mineral tones, backlit alabaster and striking macramé lend the space, which grows moody by dusk, its understated luxury. A lovely stone-floored terrace adds an Italianate slant (Guido Stefanoni led the design team), and smart touches such as burgundy-toned glasses by Hermès and woven metal placemats abound. We recommend the tables near the open kitchen, from where emerges an array of Manhattan-esque bistro fare, with grills, baked pastas and paper-thin pizzas being among the house specialties.
*MJ building, Sinsa-dong, Kangnam-gu, T 512 1046, www.gramercykitchen.com*

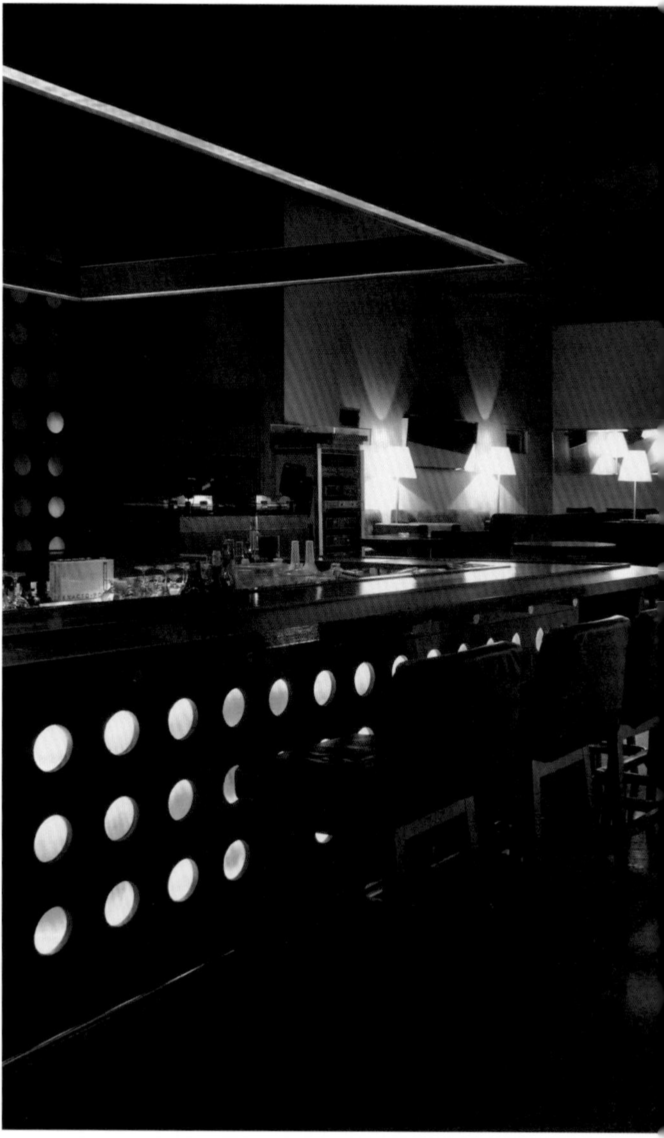

## S Bar

Perhaps the longest-established hot spot south of the Han River – one with any consistent cachet, that is .– S Bar feels by turns urbane and clubby. Done out in mainly beige tones, with lines of banquettes and small constellations of couches, the rectangular space focuses on a free-standing square bar, where the energy of the crowd is concentrated. Interaction among strangers, something that's a rare phenomenon in Korea at large, is commonplace here. In fact, on most week nights, S Bar is not much more than a neighbourly watering hole (the self-applied title 'wine bar' is perhaps stretching it). But on weekends, especially, it transforms into an ultra-lounge and door policies do come into effect.
*83-15 Cheongdam-dong, Kangnam-gu,*
*T 546 2713*

**Above Bar**

Slipped down a sliver of an alley behind the Hamilton Hotel, the upscale Above Bar represents a turning point for Itaewon nightlife, drawing a confidently stylish and youthful crowd from the Kangnam-gu area. Between the bar at one end and the spot-lit DJ booth at the other is plenty of open seating, with tones of black, silver, charcoal and amber used throughout the space. During the summer, the doors swing open to allow for people-watching. An eclectic, modern menu caters to soy-sauce Western tastes, but it is the lengthy list of cocktails, wine and vintage champagnes that gets our vote.
*119-25 Itaewon-dong, Yongsan-gu,*
*T 749 0717*

## Miss Park

Before you go, obtain directions from someone in the know – googling 'Miss Park' will get you precisely nowhere. The cutesy name belies the sleek space, which is tucked away on a side street. Its tiny bar opens onto a room that's softly lit by local standards and part-partitioned here and there to suggest privacy. Late into the night, servers who really seem to enjoy their job deliver delicious Korean dishes, just the stuff for soothing stomachs that contain one drop of *soju* too many. In short, you're sure to impress a date if you take them to Miss Park: first, because you know about it; second, because there's a lot to like about it.

*117-13 Cheongdam-dong, Kangnam-gu,*
*T 512 6333*

**WooBar**
This bar in the W Seoul (see p028) is certainly a cool space, but it can be a hit-and-miss affair. A huge stairway leads to seating in all manner of pop-gone-Seoul styles: pods, sofas, pillows and booths. Sweeping views of the Han River and the extensive list of creative, well-crafted cocktails make it well worth a visit.
*W Seoul, 21 Gwangjang-dong, Gwangjin-gu, T 2022 0333*

# INSIDER'S GUIDE

## CHI MIGGI, PARTY PROMOTER AND DESIGNER

A former model in Seoul and New York, Chi Miggi's glamorous influence now extends to the nightlife and lifestyle of her home city. Her party-promotion company, Sway, in many ways drove the city's after-hours dance-club boom, and she has now diverted some of her energies into a handbag line, Tash and Miggi, which she sells at her otherwise vintage clothing boutique Covette (see p087). A lover of food, fun and fashion, Miggi is drawn to 'the opportunities arising from living in Seoul in this exciting period of change' and to the contrasts between 'the city's sophistication and its rich cultural heritage'.

To this end, she loves to take brunch at the Park Hyatt (see p017), enjoys sipping lattes at Grand Harue (Puwon building, 95 Cheongdam-dong, T 546 9981), which has a terrace that's great for people-watching, and treats herself to a glass of champagne at the end of the working week at Tribeca (89-6 Cheongdam-dong, Kangnam-gu, T 546 1489). Miggi also likes to trawl the tree-lined streets of Garosugil (see p080) for emerging design talent as well as the scrum that is the around-the-clock Dongdaemun Market (Dongdaemun Gate) for its 'extreme' bargains. After dark, Miggi enjoys checking out the new wine bars and coffee shops popping up around Samcheong-dong or, for a big night out with friends, she club-hops between Circle (see p038) and M2 (see p040).

*For full addresses, see Resources.*

# ARCHITOUR
## A GUIDE TO SEOUL'S ICONIC BUILDINGS

Modern Seoul is gargantuan, a snarl of looping roads, elevated highways and wide avenues, with little of the old city remaining. Concrete dominates, and perhaps the iconic view of the city is of its 24 bridges that span the Han River. High-rises are surprisingly few and far between, and its architectural highlights are mainly quirky, minor works of very recent years. One of the most notable of these is Leeum, Samsung Museum of Art (see po74), a three-building, postmodernist cluster by Mario Botta, Jean Nouvel and Rem Koolhaas, whose rather varied reactions to Seoul stand as a commentary on the fractured nature of the city itself.

Koolhaas is also responsible for the lush, pastoral punch of the National University Museum of Art (see po72), which brings together nature and elemental shapes in a very local way. One of the lesser-known names, the godfather of Korean modernism, is the late Kim Swoo Geun, founder of the Space Group, whose Gyeongdong Presbyterian Church (opposite) is a bold, strange, but unforgettable snapshot of his 200-building portfolio.

Bridging Seoul's current obsessions of design and commerce is Maison Hermès (overleaf), a simply elucidated cubic structure by Rena Dumas. Further afield, it is worth taking a day trip out to the innovative Paju City (see po76) for a glimpse of what Seoul might be like were the concrete sheath to be lifted.

*For full addresses, see Resources.*

**Gyeongdong Presbyterian Church**
Said to resemble hands in prayer, this
1981 red-brick house of worship, conceived
by Kim Swoo Geun, who went on to design
the Jamsil Olympic Stadium for the 1988
Olympics, sticks closely to the modernist
code of form following function. The
second-floor entrance is reached via
a sweeping flight of shallow steps known
as The Meditator's Walk – a literal ascent
towards enlightenment. The chapel itself
is as stark as it is soaring, its bare cement
walls, an enormous cross over the altar, and
pews set at an inward angle to the central
aisle, all instilling a sense of humility.
*26-6 Jangcheung-dong 1-ga, T 2274 0161,*
*www.kdchurch.or.kr*

**Maison Hermès**

Rena Dumas's 3,000 sq m double-glass cube of shimmering, gilded strips is deceptively simple. Solid as it seems, the fashion house is hollowed out from top to bottom to form a central courtyard visible from two glassed-in sides of the interior. As well as every accessory you could possibly want, the brand temple houses a small gallery for contemporary art shows and the basement Promenade Museum, which displays objets d'art from the estate of Emile Hermès himself. Designed by former set-designer Hilton McConnico, the space is a futuristic forest of leather trees, the precious Hermès curios nestled in the trunks. Feeding Seoul's consumer fervour, Maison Hermès may be the first in a movement to rival, and maybe even outpace, Tokyo's branded architectural innovation.

*630-26 Sinsa-dong, Kangnam-gu,*
*T 542 6622, www.hermes.com*

### Incheon International Airport

Seoul's sleekest transport hub is also its largest architectural gem. Designed by US-based Fentress Architects and opened on an island in the Yellow Sea in 2001, its sweeping lines and honeycomb roof panels give it a futuristic but welcoming appearance, as do cherrywood-floored interiors by Jean-Michel Wilmotte.
*2850 Unseo-dong, Jung-gu, Incheon City, www.airport.or.kr*

**Anyang Álvaro Siza Hall**
In 2005, Portuguese architect Álvaro Siza was asked to design a structure for the entrance to the Art Park in Anyang, a satellite suburb 20km south of Seoul and home of Korea's ambitious cultural scheme, the Anyang Public Art Project. Siza accepted the commission and was joined by long-time collaborator Carlos Castanheira and Korean architect Jun-Sung Kim, masterplanner of Heyri Art Valley (see p076). The final design – a gently curved, box-shaped pavilion – exemplifies Siza's minimalist approach. The shell is made from a concrete so fine it's virtually white, while large windows illuminate the interior. Opened in 2006, it has earned Siza a loyal local following, and the same team went on to design the Mimesis Art Museum in Paju Book City (see p076). *Anyang Art Park, Manan-gu, Anyang 2-dong 5-8, Suksu 1-dong 240-9, T 03 1387 7111, apap.anyang.go.kr*

**National University Museum of Art**
Rem Koolhaas's glazed wedge structure, finished in 2005, and located near the university's main entrance, acts via its design as a model of access and exposure. Cantilevered atop a concrete block driven into the hillside, the foundation of the building parallels the slope below it, forming a roof for its pedestrian walkways. The glass exterior reveals a network of angled steel beams, reinforcing an outward sense of jointedness that gives way, inside, to one of circulation: ramps and stairwells crisscross and spiral to articulate the interconnection between the educational spaces, the library they flank and the gallery on the top level. Koolhaas's building cleverly addresses nature and urbanity, and the intense focus on driving into the future and education.
*San 56-1 Sillim 9-dong, Gwanak-gu,*
*T 880 5114*

**Leeum, Samsung Art Museum**
The three buildings that make up this museum perfectly encapsulate Seoul's ancient past (Mario Botta's Museum 1; left), postmodern present (Jean Nouvel's Museum 2; right) and nebulous future (Rem Koolhaas's Child Education & Culture Center; centre). On show is some of the world's best contemporary art. *747-18 Hannam-dong, T 2014 6900, leeum.samsungfoundation.org*

**Paju City**
An hour north of Seoul, nestled in a dell
a few miles south of the demilitarised
zone, are two innovative communities
designed as a living architecture museum.
Paju Book City (right and overleaf) is the
centre of Seoul's publishing industry,
while Heyri Art Valley was originally built
to house its workers, but has evolved into
a haphazard colony of painters, writers,
craftspeople, film-makers, musicians,
performers and architects. Very strict
architectural guidelines mean that all the
buildings, from sculpted-concrete homes
to the black-steel-clad Youlhwadang
Publishing House (right), rely on materials
– plywood, polycarbonate, copper and
glass – that reflect the contours and
colours of the surrounding countryside.
Such a commitment lends harmony to
the development as a whole and allows
it to blend with its environment.
*Gyeonggi-do, www.pajubookcity.org*

# SHOPPING

## THE BEST RETAIL THERAPY AND WHAT TO BUY

Perhaps the only thing that can match the Korean hunger for work and achievement is the pace of consumption. Beyond the big-brand meccas in Cheongdam-dong, witness Boon the Shop (see p086), an elegant monument to global-eyed Korean taste with a super-savvy clientele and interiors that wouldn't look out of place in Milan. Nearby, tiny boutiques, such as shoe vendor Suecomma Bonnie (96-5 Cheongdam-dong, Kangnam-gu, T 3443 0217) and urbanwear stop Tango de Chat (79-5 Cheongdam-dong, T 3445 4497), supply hot local brands. Department-store culture is also entrenched here; for a taste, visit Shinsegae (57-5 Chungmuro 1-ga, Jung-gu, T 727 1234) or Lotte (1 Sogong-dong, Jung-gu, T 771 2500).

Industrial product design is a national speciality, and INNO (opposite) is a don't-miss, as is a stroll through Garosugil, whose arty shops and bookstores have turned it into a hip retail haven. The spring 2008 launch that will surely fire the Seoulite thirst for design is Carla Sozzani's emporium 10 Corso Como (83-1 Soosong-dong, Jongno-gu, T 2076 7632), opening in Cheongdam-dong. For a glimpse of the old Korea, saunter down Insadong and up the pathways of Ssamziegil, the traditional crafts area where stores specialise in métiers like pottery. Then head to the mad, 24-hour Namdaemun Market (Namdaemunno, Jung-gu), whose one-off and knock-off stalls keep shoppers hooked until dawn.
*For full addresses, see Resources.*

**INNO Design**

Korean mega-brands have been slowly overtaking their Japanese counterparts in the global technological race, and design has been their key selling point. One of the unwritten stories is the small cluster of studios that has been their creative support system – INNO being one of the stand-outs. CEO and founder Kim Young-Se's effect can be measured in the billions of dollars, as his inventions include iRiver's MP3 players, Samsung phones, bottles for cosmetics range La Neige, and even shoes. INNO's Seoul store is not only a one-stop shop for tomorrow's it-devices, but a sort of archive revealing how the city has transformed itself from old to bold and new in just a few years. *INNO Tower 11-13F, Nonhyun-dong, Kangnam-gu, T 3445 6481, www.innodesign.com*

### Minetani

One of South Korea's most abundant natural resources is precious and semi-precious stones, and you'll come across plenty of cheap (but bland) jewellery stores as you explore Seoul's shopping districts. If you are looking for something a cut above, head to Minetani, a fine jewellery line set up by mother-and-daughter team Young Mee Ahn and Victoria Kim. Influenced by various styles of antique European jewellery, Minetani's pieces feature diamonds, sapphires and topaz; their most popular order is a pair of tiered white topaz earrings. The interior of their boutique exudes a minimalist cool, with its pristine white sofas, granite floors and sleek wooden display cabinets and is the perfect lure for their socialite clientele. *1st floor, Shingsegae department store, 52-5 Chungmuro 1-ga, Jung-gu, T 2310 5384*

## Mogool

Among the many fashion obsessions of Seoulites, it's probably their love of hats (especially for women, but also for men) that stands out. There are as many, if not more, chains of hat designers as there are for accessories such as shoes and bags. While many tend towards the zany and look at me designs, Mogool breaks the mould more often than most by keeping its colour palette subdued or monochromatic. Teens shop here for the edgier styles that appeal to hip-hop fans, and there's a small following for some of its classic shapes, such as the fedora. *Garosugil/Ssamziegil, T 3445 6264, www.mogool.co.kr*

### Teumi and Soos

The rapid urbanisation of Seoul has seen its inhabitants develop a growing passion for vintage furniture. As with clothes, cars and art, price has proved no object and there has been a zealous pursuit of iconic Western designs. Enter Teumi and Soos, a gallery-cum-store that helps feed the demand with its excellent exhibitions and flawless service. Wander in and you may come across a show of classics by Gio Ponti, for example, displayed with a sense of reverence that borders on the religious. At any one time, the Cheongdam-dong shop, which is flanked by the likes of Gucci and Hermès, may also offer pieces by Verner Panton, Charles and Ray Eames, and Marc Newson. Staff are knowledgeable and have an attention to detail that very much signals Seoul's arrival on the global shopping and design scenes.
*97-19 Cheongdam-dong, Kangnam-gu,*
*T 511 7305*

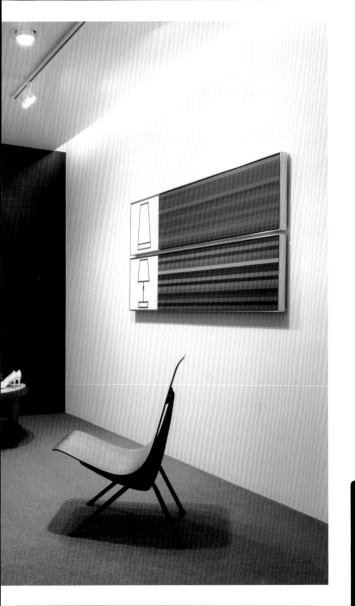

### Boon the Shop

The queen bee among this area's clutch of high-end stores, Boon the Shop, which doubles as art gallery, is a regular pitstop for Seoul's most discerning and demanding shoppers. The subtly lit and amber-hued interiors, and four floors of well-edited labels, including clothes and accessories by Matthew Williamson, Alexander McQueen and Manolo Blahnik, put Boon up there with stores such as Colette and Villa Moda. Downstairs there's a sliver of a café, where Boon's impeccably groomed clientele perch for *panini*, salads, cupcakes and green-tea lattes. The nearby branch, Boon the Shop for Men (T 3445 2841), is just as stylishly kitted out and draws a similarly well-dressed set of customers. *Sandos building, 82-3 Cheongdam-dong, Kangnam-gu, T 542 8006, www.boontheshop.com*

#### Covette

Run by the glamorous former model and style maven Chi Miggi (see p062), and the store's co-owner Tashiana Kim, Covette offers a selection of vintage clothing curated for the contemporary South Korean fashion scene and Seoul's up-to-the-minute aesthetics. The place is stuffed with tempting goods, from classic rock tees to vintage Missoni kaftans, as well as pieces by Tash and Miggi, the owners' own line of covetable leather bags; look out for the clutches and slouchy totes. Unlike many boutiques in Seoul, which show off a tiny range of products in a cold, high-design space, Covette is warm and inviting. The store is also conveniently located near some of the city's hippest *soju* bars and after-hours lounges, should you need a post-shopping reviver.
*646-7 Sinsa-dong, Kangnam-gu, T 541 6534*

# SPORTS AND SPAS
## WORK OUT, CHILL OUT OR JUST WATCH

The years 1988 and 2002 mark Seoul's emergence and arrival on the world stage, being the respective dates the city hosted the Olympics and FIFA World Cup. Koreans have long been obsessed with health, but it is largely within the last decade that a similar passion for sport has emerged. Should any national team event be on during your trip, book immediately, before local fans beat you to it. Top-level baseball is a regular fixture, and our top-choice venue is the Jamsil Stadium (see p092), designed in the shape of a traditional Korean percussion instrument. The World Cup Stadium (Sangam-dong, Mapo-gu, T 2128 2000) is home to FC Seoul and has a mall, market and fitness centre on site.

If participation is more your thing, the 20-year-old Olympic Park (overleaf) in the Songpa-gu district is wearing well. Whether you prefer to jog, stroll, sprint or rollerblade, whisking through the vast wooded area, which contains more than 200 sculptures and the 3rd-century Mongchon Fortress, is exhilarating.

The local spa and sauna culture is not to be missed, and the lively Chunjiyun (B/F Sunshine building, 11-1 Chungmuro 2-ga, T 318 8011) is a good place to head for a traditional Korean scrub and steam. For Western treatments, there is the coolly tranquil Away Spa at the W Seoul (opposite) or the calming Zen and rich-wood surroundings of the Park Hyatt's Park Club Spa (see p094). *For full addresses, see Resources.*

### Away Spa

The jaw-droppingly gorgeous interior design of the W Seoul (see p028) forms an appropriate backdrop for the above-and-beyond performance of its spa. While the hotel grounds boast tennis courts, jogging trails, two pools and a driving range, the Away Spa offers spinning, yoga, Pilates and tai-chi classes, as well as an admirable array of mind-body boosters. With a Turkish bath, hydrotherapy baths, indoor jacuzzis, a sauna and 17 treatment rooms, not to mention staff trained in hammam and Ayurvedic techniques as well as Western treatments, guests can indulge in everything from *watsu* sessions and Thai massages to seaweed wraps and jade facials. The spa also boast a rooftop deck and the Tonic café and juice bar.
*W Seoul, 21 Gwangjang-dong, Gwangjin-gu, T 2022 0450, www.starwoodhotels.com*

**Olympic Park**
Ranging over 150 hectares, myriad
monuments and sports facilities (tennis
courts, a velodrome, a swimming pool)
make the Olympic Park a major draw.
Architectural treats include the Baejke-
era Mongchon Fortress, the 24m-high
winged World Peace Gate (pictured)
and a spectacular sculpture garden.
*88-8 Bangih-dong, Songpa-gu,*
*T 410 1114, www.sosfo.or.kr*

**Jamsil Stadium**

Whether it's a remnant from WWII-era interaction or simply a shared passion with the US, Japan and Taiwan, Korea is one of the few countries outside the Americas with a passion for baseball. For seekers of interesting lines and epic scale, the country's stadiums are fascinating to visit. Resembling the form of a *janggo*, Jamsil Stadium opened in 1982, when the country's first professional baseball league, the KBO, was established. Two of the KBO's eight teams – the LG Twins and the Doosan Bears – call this 30,500-capacity local landmark home. Unlike in the US, tickets are relatively easy to come by; the Korean Series kicks off in October. *10 Jamsil-dong, Songpa-gu, T 1644 0211*

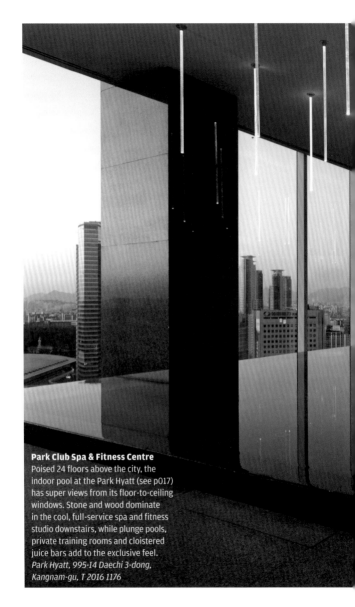

**Park Club Spa & Fitness Centre**
Poised 24 floors above the city, the
indoor pool at the Park Hyatt (see p017)
has super views from its floor-to-ceiling
windows. Stone and wood dominate
in the cool, full-service spa and fitness
studio downstairs, while plunge pools,
private training rooms and cloistered
juice bars add to the exclusive feel.
*Park Hyatt, 995-14 Daechi 3-dong,
Kangnam-gu, T 2016 1176*

# ESCAPES

## WHERE TO GO IF YOU WANT TO LEAVE TOWN

Seoulites escape the urban grind by heading out of the city to experience the extremes of nature that surround it, such as the ski resort of Yongpyong (see p102) and the raw beauty of Jeju island – Korea's answer to Hawaii – an hour south of the Korean peninsula by plane, or an overnight trip by ferry. This subtropical volcanic outcrop is dominated by Mount Hallasan, the highest peak in South Korea, and features an amazing array of lava caves and craters. While the major attraction is Mount Hallasan National Park (opposite), natural wonders aren't all the island has to offer. Top-notch restaurants, museums, shops and casinos (some of which cater exclusively to foreigners), not to mention choice hotels such as The Shilla Jeju (see p098) in the Jungmun Resort complex on the south coast, complete the idyll. The island's golf courses and beaches teem with sun-worshippers, celebrities and honeymooners alike, and add another dimension to South Korea's ambitions to be a Singapore/Hong Kong-style destination.

From Jeju, catch a ferry to Korea's southernmost spot, Marado, a small, sweet potato-shaped basalt island. This rocky, treeless hideaway is a natural monument, famous for its unique marine life. Visitors here can embrace ecotourism and stay with one of the island's 90 inhabitants in a *minbak* (b&b), and experience a rural South Korean way of life completely at odds with that of Seoul. *For full addresses, see Resources.*

**Mount Hallasan National Park, Jeju**
This dormant volcano was designated a national park in 1970 to protect its rare plant and animal species. Don't pass up the opportunity to stretch your legs on one of the four well-developed climbing routes that scale the mountain, although only two lead to Hallasan's sky-piercing 1,950m peak; the 368 smaller peaks (volcanic cinder cones) that surround it are also worth exploring. The park attracts budding entomologists and botanists, as it is famous for a vertical ecosystem comprised of thousands of species of flora and fauna.
*Seogwipo-si, Jeju-do*

**The Shilla Jeju**
Set on a private 8.5-hectare perch on
top of a cliff overlooking the Pacific at
the centre of the Jungmun Resort, this
sparkling-white fantasy hotel is a true
tropical paradise on Jeju's south coast.
Beyond its Mediterranean-style façade lie
spacious interiors that combine modern
and traditional Korean design elements;
its indoor and outdoor pools, botanic
gardens and manicured golf courses form
a perfect playground for guests who have
included Bill Clinton and numerous big-
name PGA golfers. Diners have a choice
of six restaurants and bars, including
the traditional Korean Cheonjee and
the European-style Ollae bar. To top it
all, The Shilla Jeju is home to Asia's first
Guerlain Spa. Also on the premises are
a casino and a small shopping arcade.
*3039-2 Saekdal-dong, Seogwipo-si, Jeju-
do, T 06 4735 5114, www.shilla.net/jeju*

**Yeomiji Arboretum, Jeju**
This spectacular botanical garden and greenhouse in the Jungmun Resort (see p098) nurtures more than 3,500 plants, many very rare. A train shuttles visitors between the gardens and greenhouse, and there is an observation platform 38m up offering panoramic views of the arboretum and Marado island (see p096). *Jungmun Resort, 2920 Saekdal-dong, Seogwipo-si, Jeju-do*

**Yongpyong Resort**

Only a couple of hours' drive from Seoul, this winter wonderland boasts fantastic facilities and is at the forefront of Korea's developing ski industry. Located at the foot of Balwang Mountain, Dragon Valley (as it's also known) attracts winter sports enthusiasts from mid-November until early April. The Yongpyong Resort is well known in Europe for hosting international challenges, such as the World Cup and the Winter Asian Games. There is also plenty going on in the summer, and dotting the 27 slopes of the 1,700-hectare complex are hotels, golf courses, bowling alleys, swimming pools, racquetball courts, and Japanese and Western restaurants.

*Yongsan-ri, Doam-myeon, Pyeongchang-gun, Gangwon-do, T 03 3335 5757*

# NOTES
## SKETCHES AND MEMOS

# RESOURCES

## CITY GUIDE DIRECTORY

### A

**Above Bar** 058
*119-25 Itaewon-dong*
*Yongsan-gu*
*T 749 0717*

**Actually** 045
*118-1 Cheongdam-dong*
*Kangnam-gu*
*T 3445 1350*

**Anyang Álvaro Siza Hall** 070
*Anyang Art Park*
*Manan-gu*
*Anyang 2-dong 5-8*
*Suksu 1-dong 240-9*
*T 03 1387 7111*
*apap.anyang.go.kr*

**Arario Gallery** 036
*149-2 Sogyeok-dong*
*Jongno-gu*
*T 723 6190*
*www.ararioseoul.com*

**Ariake** 046
*2nd Floor*
*The Shilla*
*202 Jangchung-dong 2-ga*
*Jung-gu*
*T 2230 3356*
*www.shilla.net*

**Away Spa** 089
*W Seoul*
*21 Gwangjang-dong*
*Gwangjin-gu*
*T 2022 0450*
*www.starwoodhotels.com*

### B

**Bamboo House** 032
*658-10 Yeoksam-dong*
*Kangnam-gu*
*T 555 6390*

**Bar 19** 044
*545-19 Sinsa-dong*
*Kangnam-gu*
*T 543 4319*

**Boon the Shop** 086
*Sandos building*
*82-3 Cheongdam-dong*
*Kangnam-gu*
*T 542 8006*
*www.boontheshop.com*

**Boon the Shop For Men** 086
*79-13 Cheongdam-dong*
*Kangnam-gu*
*T 3445 2841*
*www.boontheshop.com*

### C

**Cafe** 035
*Kukje Gallery*
*59-1 Sogyeok-dong*
*Jongno-gu*
*T 735 8441*
*www.kukjegallery.com*

**Café Mou** 050
*650-9 Park View building*
*Sinsa-dong*
*Kangnam-gu*
*T 3444 6069*
*www.cafemou.co.kr*

**Cheongwadae** 033
*Gyeongbokgung Palace*
*1 Sejong-no*
*Jongno-gu*
*T 737 5800*

**The Chinese Restaurant** 026
*Grand Hyatt*
*747-7 Hannam 2-dong*
*Yongsan-ku*
*T 799 8164*
*www.seoul.grand.hyatt.com*

# HOTELS

## ADDRESSES AND ROOM RATES

**Fraser Suites** 016
Room rates:
One-bedroom apartment, KRW220,000;
Four-bedroom apartment, KRW357,000
*72 Nakwon-dong*
*Jongno-gu*
*T 6262 8888*
*seoul.frasershospitality.com*

**Grand Hyatt** 026
Room rates:
double, from KRW228,000;
Grand Club Room, from KRW283,000
*747-7 Hannam 2-dong*
*Yongsan-ku*
*T 797 1234*
*seoul.grand.hyatt.com*

**Imperial Palace** 024
Room rates:
double, KRW228,000;
Executive Suite, KRW353,000;
Royal Suite, from KRW6,000,000
*248-7 Nonhyeon-dong*
*Kangnam-gu*
*T 3440 8000*
*www.imperialpalace.co.kr*

**Millennium Hilton** 020
Room rates:
double, KRW189,000;
Executive 'e' Room, from KRW300,000
*395 Namdaemun-ro 5-ga*
*Jung-gu*
*T 753 7788*
*www.hilton.co.kr*

**Park Hyatt** 017
Room rates:
double, KRW444,000;
Diplomatic Suite, from KRW4,100,000
*995-14 Daechi 3-dong*
*Kangnam-gu*
*T 2016 1234*
*seoul.park.hyatt.com*

**The Ritz-Carlton** 027
Room rates:
double, KRW433,000;
Prime Deluxe Room, KRW433,000;
Presidential Suite, from KRW4,660,000
*602 Yeoksam-dong*
*Kangnam-gu*
*T 3451 8000*
*www.ritzcarlton.com*

**The Shilla** 016
Room rates:
double, KRW377,000
*202 Jangchung-dong 2-ga*
*Jung-gu*
*T 2233 3131*
*www.shilla.net*

**The Shilla Jeju** 098
Room rates:
double, KRW383,000
*3039-2 Saekdal-dong*
*Seogwipo-si*
*Jeju-do*
*T 06 4735 5114*
*www.shilla.net/jeju*

**Somerset Palace** 022
Room rates:
Studio, KRW172,000;
One-Bedroom Apartment, KRW188,900;
One Bedroom Executive Apartment,
from KRW385,000
*85 Susong-dong*
*Jongno-gu*
*T 6730 8888*
*www.somerset.com*

**W Seoul** 028
  Room rates:
  double, KRW522,000;
  Mega Room, KRW610,000;
  Cool Corner Room, from KRW3,850,000;
  Extreme Wow Suite, KRW8,100,000
  *21 Gwangjang-dong*
  *Gwangjin-gu*
  *T 465 2222*
  *www.starwoodhotels.com*
**The Westin Chosun** 016
  Room rates:
  double, KRW333,000
  *87 Sogong-dong*
  *Jung-gu*
  *T 771 0500*
  *www.starwoodhotels.com*

## WALLPAPER* CITY GUIDES

**Editorial Director**
Richard Cook

**Art Director**
Loran Stosskopf
**City Editor**
Rob McKeown
**Editor**
Rachael Moloney
**Executive**
**Managing Editor**
Jessica Firmin
**Travel Bookings Editor**
Sara Henrichs

**Chief Designer**
Daniel Shrimpton
**Designer**
Lara Collins
**Map Illustrator**
Russell Bell

**Photography Editor**
Christopher Lands
**Photography Assistant**
Robin Key

**Chief Sub-Editor**
Jeremy Case
**Sub-Editor**
Melanie Parr
**Editorial Assistant**
Ella Marshall

**Interns**
Rosa Bertoli
Francesca Wilson

**Wallpaper* Group**
**Editor-in-Chief**
Tony Chambers
**Publisher**
Neil Sumner

**Contributors**
Meirion Pritchard
Ellie Stathaki
Glenn Tanner

Wallpaper* ® is a
registered trademark
of IPC Media Limited

All prices are correct at
time of going to press,
but are subject to change.

## PHAIDON

**Phaidon Press Limited**
Regent's Wharf
All Saints Street
London N1 9PA

**Phaidon Press Inc**
180 Varick Street
New York, NY 10014

Phaidon® is a registered
trademark of Phaidon
Press Limited

www.phaidon.com

First published 2008
© 2008 IPC Media Limited

ISBN 978 0 7148 4751 1

A CIP Catalogue record for
this book is available from
the British Library.

Printed in China

## PHOTOGRAPHERS

**Dbimages/Alamy**
Seoul city view,
inside front cover

**Marc Gerritsen**
Jongno Tower, p012
Somerset Palace,
p022, p023
Imperial Palace,
pp024-025
Grand Hyatt, p026
Gyeongbokgung
Palace, p033
Kukje and Hyundai
galleries, p034, p035
Arario Gallery, pp036-037
Circle, pp038-039
The Gaon, p041
Naos Nova, pp042-043
Bar 19, p044
Actually, p045
Diner Kraze, pp048-049
Café Mou, p050
Vinga, p051
The Timber House,
pp052-053
Gramercy Kitchen,
pp054-055
S Bar, pp056-057
Above Bar, p058
Miss Park, p059
Gyeongdong Presbyterian
Church, p065
Incheon International
Airport, pp068-069

INNO Design, p081
Minetani, p082
Mogool, p083
Teumi and Soos,
pp084-085
Boon the Shop, p086
Covette, p087
Park Club Spa & Fitness
Centre, pp094-095

**Fernando Guerra**
Anyang Álvaro Siza Hall,
pp070-071

**Hong Jang Hyun**
Chi Miggi, p063

**ImageGap/Alamy**
Jamsil Stadium,
pp092-093

**JTB Photo/Photolibrary**
Yeomiji Arboretum, Jeju
pp100-101

**Mixa Co, Ltd/Alamy**
N Seoul Tower, pp010-011

**Masao Nishikawa**
Maison Hermès,
pp066-067

**Christopher Sturman**
Galleria, pp014-015
Leeum, Samsung Art
Museum, pp074-075

**TongRo Image Stock/Alamy**
Mount Hallasan National
Park, Jeju, p097

**Patrick Voigt**
National University Museum
of Art, pp072-073
Paju City, pp076-077,
pp078-079

**WizData Inc/Alamy**
Olympic Park, pp090-091

# SEOUL
## A COLOUR-CODED GUIDE TO THE HOT 'HOODS

### MYEONG-DONG
Shopping and a quirky cluster of buildings draw all-comers to the city's financial heart

### APGUJEONG
Sample a true taste of K-culture in the neon-lit concept stores and buzzy back streets

### SAMCHEONG-DONG
Upmarket bars and sleek eateries are springing up fast in this leafy residential enclave

### HONGDAE
This off-centre district is proving a hub for the city's burgeoning art and club scene

### ITAEWON
An eclectic mix of chichi bars and gay clubs now inhabit this former expat ghetto

### CHEONGDAM-DONG
Seoul's answer to Beverly Hills is the place to come for your designer labels and latte fix

For a full description of each neighbourhood, see the Introduction.
Featured venues are colour-coded, according to the district in which they are located.